THE SAAS SALES METHOD FUNDAMENTALS

HOW TO HAVE CUSTOMER CONVERSATIONS

BY JACCO VAN DER KOOIJ
AND DOMINIQUE LEVIN

Edited by Fernando Pizarro and Dan Smith

Revision 5.0

ISBN-13: 978-1986270205

ISBN-10: 1986270203

Winning by Design LLC
San Francisco, California
United States of America
For more information, visit www.winningbydesign.com

More from Winning by Design

The SaaS Sales Method Fundamentals: How to Have Customer Conversations is part of Winning by Design's Sales Blueprints series. Other books in the series include:

The SaaS Sales Method: The Science and Process of Sales

Blueprints for a SaaS Sales Organization: How to Design, Build and Scale a Customer-Centric Sales Organization

The SaaS Sales Method for Sales Development Representatives: How to Prospect for Customers

The SaaS Sales Method for Account Executives: How to Win Customers

The SaaS Sales Method for Customer Success & Account Managers: How to Grow Customers

Contents

Introduction

Regardless of what whiz-bang technology you choose to reach your customers, what you say and how you say it is still the most important part of customer engagement. The purpose of this book is to help you learn what to say and how to say it through practice and application.

The skills you learn in this book will help you in everything you do as a sales professional, and we will refer back to them often as we build out sales blueprints going forward.

NOTE: These books are meant to get dirty! We encourage you to write in them, do the exercises, dog ear the pages, and anything else that will help you interact with the content.

1. Communication

Nobody cares how much you know...

...until they know how much you care

– Theodore Roosevelt

Before you start engaging with your customer, you must master three basic elements:

- Know what a customer-centric methodology is: Putting yourself in their shoes, and starting conversations always keeping this in mind.

- Understand your customer: Do your research – understand their role, their persona, their industry, and the specific use-cases and customer stories that will help you relate to them.

- Be a customer-centric professional: Show up every day on time, energized and ready to perform. Your workplace both online (LinkedIn) and in the real world need to be set up to help you and your customer succeed.

To engage a customer, we use these elements:

1. We string six forms of Interactions together...

2. ...into Sequences that are applied across stages (such as Prospecting, Winning, and Growing)...

3. ...into a series of sales plays...

4. ...resulting in a series of meetings.

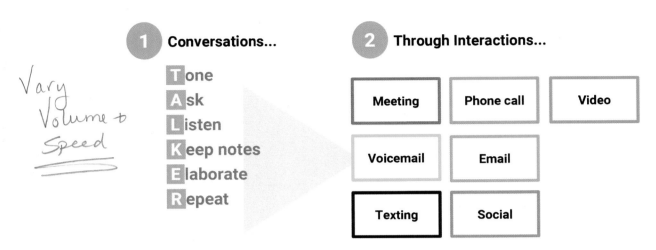

Figure 1: Great conversations happen through different interactions

In Figure 1, you can see how key conversation techniques can be applied in 6 different kinds of interactions, which in turn can be applied to sales development, sales, customer success, and account management.

Table 1.1 Interactions you need to excel at as a sales professional

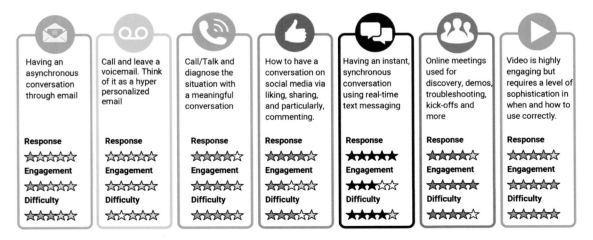

1.1 Winning By Design Communication Technique

During the sales process, you are communicating with your customer. This requires that you become a specialist in communicating outside your age bracket, outside your culture, and beyond. You have to learn how to communicate with anyone/anytime. Below are 9 keys to customer-centric communication.

T **Tone** of voice

A **Ask** questions

L **Listen** to what your client says

K **Keep notes** and include your customer's tone words

E **Elaborate** by digging deeper with the intent to understand

R **Repeat** back what you have learned

1.1.1 Tone of Voice

In a phone call, your voice is the most powerful tool of all, and it is an instrument you need to learn how to play. If you are able to understand the power of tone, you can translate it into email and text messages.

Julian Treasure
How to speak so that people want to listen
6.9M views · Jun 2014

Credit: Julian Treasure and TED

Google search or type: http:// goo.gl/Dd2gCN

ACTION: Identify the different ways to control your voice. What are they?

1. ....

2. ....

3. ....

4. ....

5. ....

1.1.2   Ask Questions

The ABCs of Customer-Centric Communication:

Always Be Curious

– JACCO VAN DER KOOIJ

When you are on the phone with a customer, it hurts you to start selling straight away, like so many sales professionals feel they have to. Great sales professionals start by asking questions to diagnose the situation, without mentioning the company they work for or service they sell.

Through the art of questioning, they determine where the prospect has pain. Once the pain is identified, then they can determine the severity (priority).

For example, imagine that you are an off-duty doctor who sees someone limping. Before you are able to offer a recommendation of using a cast or just using pain medication, you must understand what happened and assess their circumstances. If you just start telling them what to do (or worse, starting to examine them without establishing your credibility as a doctor first), they will not be open to the help you are trying to offer them.

 **PRO TIP** The fastest way to earn someone's trust is to provide valuable insight and establish yourself as an expert by asking the right kind of questions.

– DAN SMITH

Question-based selling is simply the most powerful way to understand the customer's real pains, if there is a critical event, and the impact it has on their business.

Here's how it works;

- Questions that control the speed of a conversation: Open-ended vs. Closed-ended Questions.

- Questions that control quality of a conversation: Situational vs. Pain Questions.

SPEED of the conversation

People find it a lot easier to respond to *are you hungry?* vs. *why are you hungry?* The first one can be answered by a single word (in this case yes/no) which is called a closed-ended question, and the second requires you to elaborate which is called an open-ended question. Think of the speed of the conversation as a car with stick shift. There are gears you can (and sometimes have to) shift through. There are four gears you can use to ask questions.

Four gears of questions to control speed

1 Closed
2 Closed + Context
3 Open
4 Open + Context

Figure 2: The 4 ways to change speed of conversation with questions

Closed-ended Questions	Open-ended Questions
Usually receives a single word or very short, factual answer. For example, "How many people work for you?" The answer is "6"; "What is your title?" etc. Closed-ended questions often get a short response. They are important to open and close conversations.	Requires longer answers; open-ended questions require the customer to contribute knowledge on the topic, and better yet, an opinion. They usually begin with asking, why do you do this..., how are you doing that..., and what are your plans for...
Without context: Are you the VP of Sales? **With Context:** I notice on LinkedIn that you are the VP of Sales; did I get that right?	**Without context:** What is keeping you up at night? **With Context:** People I spoke to say that they have issues with ___ and ___. May I ask what are the key issues you run into?

Best used to:

- Start up a conversation.

- Establish the base situation:

  "How many employees?"

  "Where are your teams located?"

- Get an honest answer at a critical moment:

  "Are you ready to move forward?"

- Setting up a conversation:

  "Are you happy with your provider?"

Best used to:

- Speed up a conversation as the customer gets comfortable:

  "How is your current process for..."

- Identifying the impact:

  "What would happen to your business if you ..."

- Establishing a value proposition:

  "What would 10% more mean..."

`PRO TIP` If you find your customer not very responsive/engaged in the conversation, you probably are asking a lot of closed-ended questions. Try asking a simple open-ended question.

`PRO TIP` Asking repetitive why/how questions gets boring quickly. Change it up with more conversational questions, such as "May I ask how..." and "Can you describe..."

`SPEED` Shifting gears

You can use a closed-ended questions (gear 1) to prompt an answer for an open-ended question (gear 2)

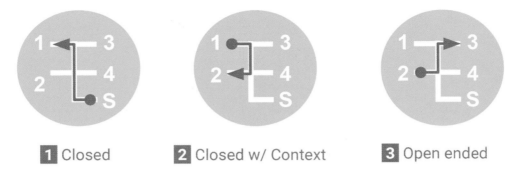

1 Closed   **2** Closed w/ Context   **3** Open ended

Figure 3: Examples of shifting between questions

GOOD EXAMPLE: **Shifting gears**

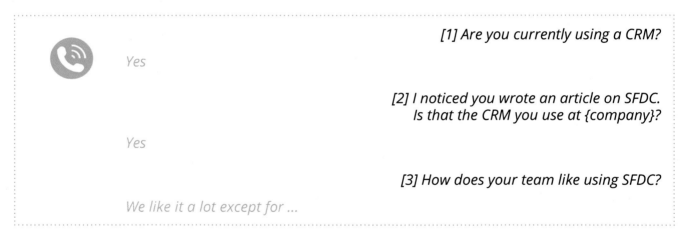

You can use a close ended questions (gear 1) to prompt an answer for an open-ended question (gear 2).

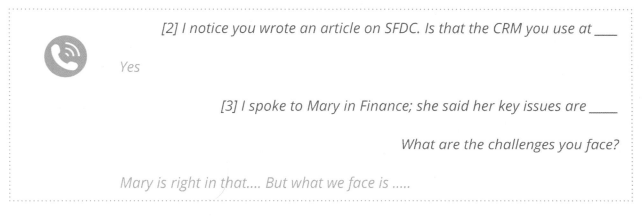

[2] I notice you wrote an article on SFDC. Is that the CRM you use at ___

Yes

[3] I spoke to Mary in Finance; she said her key issues are ____

What are the challenges you face?

Mary is right in that.... But what we face is .....

QUALITY of the questions

To manage quality we differentiate between three different kind of questions:

Situational **Question**   Pain **Question**   Impact **Question**

Situational questions: "How many offices do you have?"

Situational questions deal with facts about the customer's existing circumstances. Because they usually give you simple background information, they are often close-ended. These questions are used to understand: 1) if the customer is qualified, 2) their level of understanding of their own problem, and 3) how much knowledge they have about potential solutions.

Although asking ten of these in a row sounds like a game of "20 Questions" – or worse, an interrogation – when used properly, they can make you sound like an expert by setting the stage and demonstrating you've done your research. Prospects can then infer that you can help them solve real problems.

 **PRO TIP** Thoughtful situational questions are key! But be careful: the problem with asking too many situational questions in a row will make the customer feel like they are being grilled. Not a good experience. You can avoid this by adding your own insight and turning it more into a conversation, but also eliciting your customer to provide more detailed feedback.

- JACCO VAN DER KOOIJ

Aim to ask 3-5 great situational questions for every qualification call, or every discovery call to confirm that your research is accurate or if their circumstances have changed since your last conversation. Here is a typical situational question:

GOOD EXAMPLE: A simple situational question

 *Twenty-four*
How many people do you have on your sales team?

If this does not reflect your research, you can ask a situational question, inviting a customer into a conversation by reflecting you have done your homework.

I noticed on LinkedIn there are 20 sales people working out of your New York office. Did I get that right?

Yes, that's right.

And I noticed 2 new job openings. Does this mean you have 22 people on your team?

Close. When you add SalesOps it gets to 25.

P ain Questions: "What pains or challenges are you experiencing?"

Pain questions are where you find the pain, or the challenges, that they are experiencing. This should be a solid portion of your calls. If you haven't built trust through providing value, they will give you a high-level generic answer like "Of course the business needs more revenue." But if you've asked a series of 3-5 strong situational questions, now it's time to drill into the good stuff. Reference what you have already learned in (S), and make it relevant to your customer.

Do not bring up your product or solution. It's too early to begin "selling."

You have to earn the right to prescribe a solution through proper diagnosis. These questions are about them; both for their business, and to establish personal priorities. If they tell you they just raised a round of funding and are planning to build out the sales team, find out how they will share best practices with the new reps to ramp quickly.

BAD EXAMPLE: Too cliche and insincere – avoid questions that are too broad like this one:

What keeps you up at night?

This question has been over-used, and is too general. Your customer may respond by saying that his newborn is keeping him/her up.

GOOD EXAMPLE: **Let's make it a little more granular...**

What are your biggest challenges with the sales team?

BETTER EXAMPLE: **Even more granular...**

What are your biggest challenges with having the sales team enter data in your CRM?

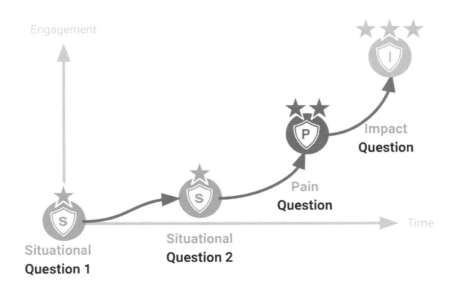

GREAT EXAMPLE: **Make it conversational, add a 3rd-party reference**

We recently met Mary X at Company Y.
She expressed that her main pain was that her sales
team was not entering data in the CRM.
They updated the CRM on the last day of the week/month.
How does your team enter data in CRM?

The last question, although more verbose (and best applied by AEs):

- Offers your customer valuable insight from a peer.

- Makes it reflect that you are an expert.

- Makes you look like you are involved in the industry.

- Establishes a way out. If this story does not resonate, you can keep providing stories without you personally getting a "rejection" (e.g., the customer can reject how other customers are making their lives better, without rejecting your product).

PRO TIP It's important to note that your customer will not give you the underlying pain and impact until you have built rapport and trust. That is something you have to earn through the conversation.

– DOMINIQUE LEVIN

GREAT EXAMPLE: Stringing together situational and pain questions

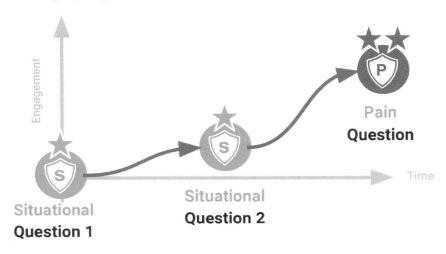

Figure 4: Building engagement through questions

EXAMPLE: Below we are stringing 2 closed-ended situational questions together leading to 2 open-ended pain questions

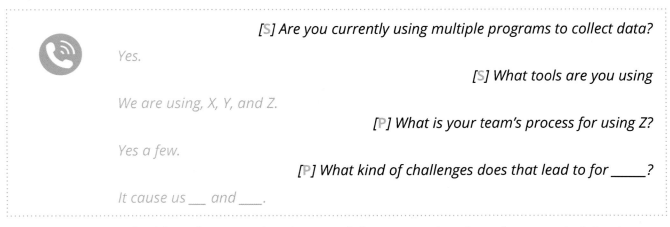

The next step is to build on the pains they have and the impact that these have on their business.

Impact Questions: Any question that explains the impact that solving the pain will have

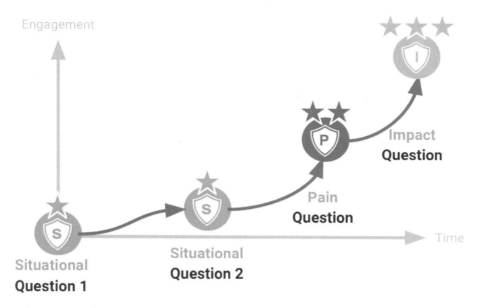

Figure 5: Ask impact questions after pain for maximum engagement

Impact questions are the meat and potatoes of a great sales conversation. Impact questions identify the impact that gets delivered by solving the pain. This will be covered in more detail in Chapter 6 when we are diagnosing a customer.

Help your customer realize the impacts to their business beyond just the symptoms of the pain, and then link the problem to other potentially bigger issues they never considered to encourage eagerness to find a solution.

When asked at the right stage of your conversation, they will unlock the door to achieving a positive outcome when using your solution. This will result in more alignment during negotiation, and a higher contract value.

Are you currently using an expense system? [S]

Yes we are.

What kind of expense system? [S]

We are using Excel spreadsheets.

Does that work for you? [P]

Well it does but it takes a lot of time.

I understand with 20 people!
How much time do you think? [V]?

It takes me about 1 day/week.

What would you do if you got that day back?

Work on other more pressing projects.

As the conversation progresses, the engagement increases. Compare this to a bad example.

BAD EXAMPLE: **Moving back to situational questions**

Are you currently using an expense system? [S1]

Yes we are.

What kind of expense system? [S2]

We are using Excel spreadsheets.

Does that work for you? [P1]

Well it does but it takes a lot of time.

How many employees do you have? [S3]

20.

Got it! Thank you.

If we draw this out, you notice how we got to the pain but never figured out what the value to the client was. The value is the impact on their business! And the impact is what they are buying.

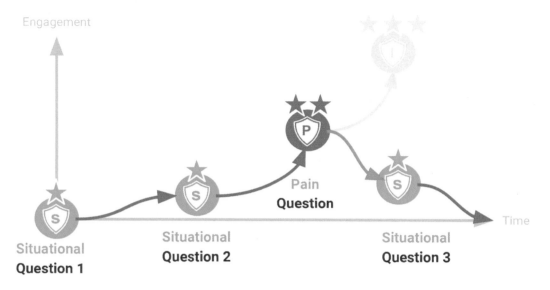

Figure 6: Asking a situational question can drop engagement at a wrong point in conversation

Instead, try to lead-in with a impact question. Below are a few examples; we recommend you make note of great impact questions specific to your business!

EXAMPLE: **Great impact lead-in questions**

What effect does that have on...

How often does that cause...

Does that ever lead to...

What is the result when...

GREAT EXAMPLE: Summarize/empathize, then ask for impact

Are you currently using an expense system? [S]

Yes we are.

What kind of expense system? [S]

We are using Excel spreadsheets.

Does that work for you? [P]

Well it does but it takes a lot of time.

I understand with 20 people!
How much time do you think? [V]?

It takes me about 1 day/week.

Okay so you have about 20 people providing you with expenses
in Excel sheets taking you about 20% or 75 days a year.
Well you are not the first. Honestly I hear this all the time!
May I ask what else could you do with that time?

Help win more deals for the company!

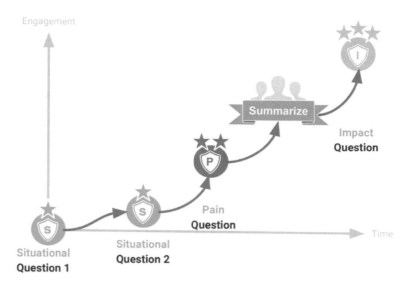

Figure 7: Impact questions are best after summarizing pain points

 **PRO TIP** Refrain from asking Impact questions before you understand the most important pains and relevant situation for the situation the customer is in. Too early, and a Impact question can come off as too aggressive and pushy. Impact questions are typically done after a few minutes of thoughtful discovery.

- DAN SMITH

Use a real customer call you have had in the last two weeks using Situational, Pain and Impact questions.

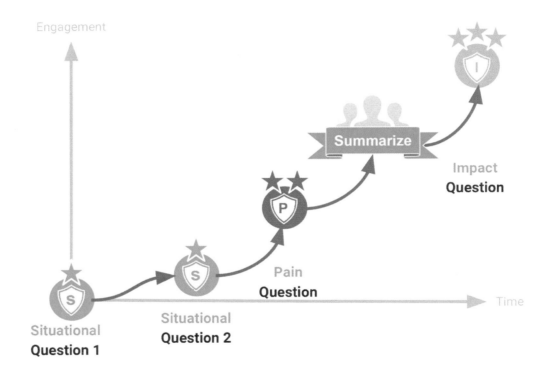

Figure 8: Impact questions after summary exercise

Call Summary	Your Notes
What is their situation?	**S1**:
	S2:
What were two of their biggest Pain points?	**P1**:
	P2:
Summarize this information in two sentences for your hand-off.	
What customer use-case could you leverage that best matches their job title, desired outcome, or similar industry?	**3rd** **Party Reference/Use-Case**
Identify the impact.	**I**:

1.1.3 **L** Listen and Mirror

Active listening is mindfully listening to your customers, building on the response they are giving, and providing cues that show them that you're actually comprehending what they are saying. But what do many salespeople do instead? They use the time that the customers are talking to bask in the moment of having asked a great question, and prepare to score another equally astonishing question.

Active listening can be done in a few specific ways: Verbal, Tone or Visual.

EXAMPLE: **Use of a verbal word that stands out and then mirroring that word**

That is of no particular interest to me.

What in particular is of interest to you?

You are mirroring your customer's specific language. This indicates to your customer that you are listening to what they have to say.

EXAMPLE: Use of tone in your voice...

- If your customer is in a hurry, you can speak just a touch faster so they know you are responding to their sense of urgency. Then you slow it down so they calm down.

- If it seems like your customer is not paying attention, you can increase the upbeat tone of your voice, and it will gain their attention, which you hear in their tone of voice.

- If your customer sounds like they are annoyed, start keeping it short to speed up the conversation, then gradually in a few sentences increase your level of excitement.

EXAMPLE: Visual cues during a conference call

- Show them that you are taking notes (screen share your notes).

- Looking into the camera, tilting your head.

- Using movements like nodding, using hands in gestures, and raising a pen into view.

1.1.4 K Keep Notes

Note-taking is a key skill that sets apart professionals from amateurs. The primary reason you need note-taking is because your brain is fooling you. Your brain is tricking you in remembering what was important to you! In customer-centric selling, note-taking is critical, as it allows you to remember what was important to your customer. Also, your memory recalls the first and last topic they mentioned, but often you will forget all the things you talked about in the middle.

BEST PRACTICES

- DO Keep it short and simple.

- DO NOT write down every word they say.

- DO use symbols; Think of (S) and (P), Priorities such as (1), (2), and arrows to show causality.

- DO note specific TONE words.

PRO TIP Sometimes because you are taking notes, your customer hears either awkward silences, or your keyboard strokes. Don't let there be a mistake that you are disengaged. Instead, call it out to let them know you are taking notes. Now every time there is a silence/keystrokes they see it as a sign you are engaged.

- Jacco van der Kooij

1.1.5 E Elaborate

Elaborating is the art of following the conversation with the intent of better understanding it.

BAD EXAMPLE: Focus on selling

There is no benefit in that feature you just talked about for me at this time.

Oh okay... let me throw something

else at the board and see if it sticks...

In this example, there were three clear signals given by the customer that a careful listener could elaborate on:

- No benefit
- What feature
- This time

There is no benefit in that feature you talked about, at this time.

Oh okay... May I ask what kind of benefit are you looking for?

There is no benefit in that feature you talked about, at this time.

Are there any specific features you are looking for?

There is no benefit in that feature you talked about, at this time.

You say at this time, is there a time when you would see

this feature making an impact for you?

You follow the conversation and elaborate with a healthy sense of curiosity.

1.1.6 R Repeat What You Heard

A customer appreciates when you listen to them. But most people only pay attention to a customer to listen if they say something that is relevant to the "seller." That is not listening. That is filtering. To let the customer know that you are listening, you repeat back what you have heard and often use the same tone words they said.

BAD EXAMPLE: Sales person listening to find more features they can sell

Manual data entry into a CRM is giving our people a headache. Two people do nothing but entering data all day. If we had automatic data entry, those people could help out with lead generation instead.

Awesome. We love to help you with that.
We also offer great Dashboards that can show that data.

In the above example, notice that it is not "Awesome" that the customer is having a headache from manual data entry from the customer's point of view. Be careful of word choice.

- **DO NOT** use crutch words such as "Awesome" when a customer just explained something negative – contain your excitement that you can help them with it.

- **DO NOT** pitch your features without knowing the impact they offer.

- **DO** repeat what you heard using their tone words.

GOOD EXAMPLE: Sales professional at work

Manual data entry into a CRM is giving our people a headache. Two people do nothing but entering data all day. If we had automatic data entry those people could help out with lead generation instead.

So if I got this right; 2 of your people are entering data manually all day using time that could be spent on leadgen instead...

Exactly.

I hear that a lot.

TALKER is the framework you should use when interacting with customers on any medium like email, phone or in-person. By understanding these core concepts through each part of your conversation with customers both at the beginning and end of their buying journey, you will come across as a true professional.

2. Email

If I Had More Time....

...I Would Wave Written a Shorter Letter

– Blaise Pascal

Writing an email is a skill. Most people are never actually trained on how to write a proper email – so we must tackle this with precision. It means not only writing a proper email, but making sure that your emails are always customer-centric. Here's how we break this down:

- **Preparing to email:** You need to do research to understand your customer.

- **Selecting valuable insights:** Offer your customer something of value to them.

- **Writing an email:** Write high quality, personalized emails.

- **Using video in your email:** Stand out and save time with a short video.

- **Measuring engagement:** Learn what works, so you can do more of what does work and stop doing what doesn't work.

2.1 Preparing to Email

If you know more about the customer and the impact of their imminent decision – and you have the right solution – you will help your customer win! This power is earned with thorough online research, which signals to your customer that you care about them.

The fact that you care opens up a door to a room full of new insights. This does not require you to do a month-long deep dive. The online world is powered by search tools, and the information you desperately seek is often laying around in plain sight.

Email Preparation Checklist

Industry-Specific	Company-Specific
☐ Finance	☐ Crunchbase
☐ Ad Tech	☐ TechCrunch
☐ Software	☐ LinkedIn (size, goal)
☐	☐ YouTube Overview Video
☐	☐ ....
☐	☐ ....

Problem-Specific	Person-Specific
☐ Google/YouTube	☐ Twitter
☐ SlideShare	☐ Facebook
☐ Company website	☐ LinkedIn profile
☐ Subscribe to their service	☐ Google Images (search for their name)
☐ Submit a "bug"	☐ ....
☐	☐ ....
☐	☐ ....

A modern sales professional, armed with WiFi connectivity will be able to research by tracking digital footprints and get a basic understanding of what is going on with the opportunity.

DO perform an advanced Google search for a company's .PPT files – most companies share content through PPTs (on Google, click Settings in the lower right corner, and then Advanced Search).

DO check out LinkedIn references – find out what the references say about the decision maker.

DO identify 2-3 competitors through Crunchbase/TechCrunch; better yet, identify a substitute!

DO schedule a briefing with your team to take them through your findings and prepare for the call.

DO include a link to your research in your email; it signals to their organization that you have done your research, which increases the chance that they will value your opinion.

2.2 Selecting Valuable Insights

Once you know the value props for the persona that you're working with, find valuable content you can share with them that either: 1) helps them be better at their job, or 2) shares insights about something someone in their role typically cares about.

Use the following exercise to identify use-cases that pertain to specific industries identified above, or content geared to specific personas (e.g., articles that grab the interest of CEOs will be different from those that grab the attention of end users).

EXERCISE: Identify use-cases that are relevant by industry or persona

	What Do You Have To Offer Your Customer? (use-case, link, etc.)	Industry or Persona?
1		
2		
3		
4		
5		
6		
7		
8		
9		
10		

2.3 Writing an Email - RRR

The key to a great customer-centric email is providing value, and resisting the urge to sell. It's not easy for every email you send to be valuable to every person you write to. But with executives receiving such a high volume of over 140 emails per day, just because you can automate emails to try and get in front of them does not mean you should.

In 2017, the total number of emails sent and received per day will exceed 269 billion on the way to reaching 306 billion by 2020.

As a sales professional, your focus must be on starting a conversation and helping your customer solve their problems. If it's too long, it won't get read. If it gets deleted before opening – that won't work either. There is both art and science in making sure you communicate effectively by email.

Instead of always aiming for "one-swing home runs" and booking a meeting in one email (prospecting), or recapping a complex conversation with a long recap (winning or growing) – focus on providing simple value-added communication.

Structure your email to evoke a desirable response

Songs, movies, books: they all have a storyline. The proper structure of an outbound email consists of the following:

R Relevance	Demonstrates research of the person or company, and references something similar.
R Reward	Offer value, such as a link to valuable insights, a relevant blog post, video etc.
R Request	Call to action based on situation (time, event, date etc.).

Do not confuse "personalization" with "relevance"

The key to helping your customer solve their problem needs to start with you providing context first. Your customers can spot emails that look like they were sent to 1,000 people very easily, even though you may have their name and company name in the email; that's not valuable to them.

Break down relevance by doing Research and referencing similar companies, customers or industries that will mean something to your customer. Context is critically important. Start-up companies don't feel very compelled to apply technology solutions just because huge enterprise companies are your customers.

Just imagine getting pitched by a sales rep asking you to consider buying pagers for communication because some of the biggest hospitals in the world use their products every today!

- **DO** keep it short. Half as long, twice as powerful.
- **DO** optimize for mobile phone. Make effective use of the subject line and the first 50 characters.
- **DO NOT** start with a "Hi my name is ... and I work for..." Instead get to the point!
- **DO NOT** start opening sentence with "I." Make it about them, not you.
- **DO** talk in the reference section not about "great feature a, b and c our service offers," but instead about "How customer X and Y experienced great benefit A and great benefit B."
- **DO** offer valuable insights.
- **DO NOT** include attachments – always link to content.
- **DO** use a person's first name in front of your request to draw their attention to a key point.
- **DO** close with a mutual social connection, such as being from the same school.
- **DO NOT** try to close with an immediate meeting – your primary goal is to gauge interest.

When writing an email, put yourself in your customer's shoes. If they don't know you already, all they care about is how you can help them solve their problems or help them look good in front of their boss.

Remember that customers make decisions emotionally first, so don't lead with rational information unless you know it will resonate with that person in particular.

 **PRO TIP** Try adding a "P.S." after you sign off – it's a super effective way to draw your customer's attention to something valuable specifically about them. Give them something unusual, but relevant. "P.S. Since you are into time management, here's an article I think you'd like."

– DOMINIQUE LEVIN

To help reinforce the importance of **R** elevance, we will break up this part of the email in two parts:

R esearch **and** **R** eference.

EXERCISE: Write an email

R esearch

....

....

R eference

....

....

R eward

....

....

R equest

....

....

Write a first draft

When first writing, you may have lots of "I-statements." That is okay to get out the initial framework and structure – we'll make better in Step 2.

Hi Laris,

R esearch   *I was looking at your LinkedIn profile this morning, and I noticed that you led the Salesforce implementation for your organization.*

R eference   *I've worked with other people with similar responsibilities to help them increase their team's Salesforce adoption.*

R eward   *I've attached a case study which shows how one of our most satisfied customers leverages _____ "Salesforce Integration" feature to help increase adoption, while making their reps more productive.*

R equest   *Could we discuss this feature in depth on Tuesday at 3 PM EST?*

STEP 2 **Apply Best Practices, in particular**

- Inspect all "I," "We," "Our," etc. Remove as many as you can.
- Add the customer's first name to the request.
- Shorten your opening by combining **Research** and **Reference**➔**Relevance.**

R elevance

....

....

R eward

....

....

R equest

....

....

GREAT EXAMPLE: Turning the "I" statements into "You"

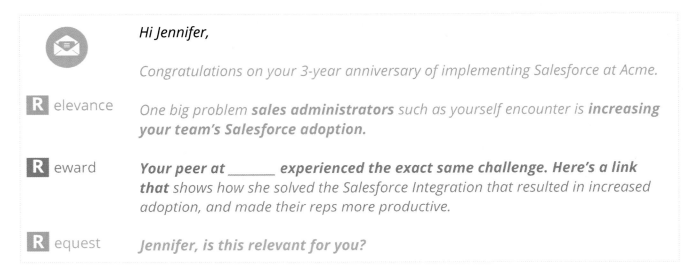

Hi Jennifer,

Congratulations on your 3-year anniversary of implementing Salesforce at Acme.

R elevance — *One big problem **sales administrators** such as yourself encounter is **increasing your team's Salesforce adoption.***

R eward — ***Your peer at _____ experienced the exact same challenge. Here's a link that** shows how she solved the Salesforce Integration that resulted in increased adoption, and made their reps more productive.*

R equest — ***Jennifer, is this relevant for you?***

STEP 3 **Create a subject line**

There is no formula or subject line advice that will work every time. Avoid using click-bait ("you'll never guess what's inside!") or deceptive ("our meeting next Tuesday at 2:30"), generic or bland "marketing-esque" subject lines.

Instead, create subject lines that spark curiosity and are relevant to the body of the message. Always test your subject lines by tracking open rates and replies.

One way to start is to pick one or two words from each sentence to make it your subject

> **Subject:** Research / Relevance / Request

Would become:

> **Subject:** Salesforce / Adoption issues / Relevant??

STEP 4 Create a strong close/call to action

Assign a task/question	Appreciate any help in answering my question
Assign a task/introduction	Thanks for pointing me in the right direction
Social close (alma mater)	Go Bruins
Social close (native tongue)	Met Vriendelijke Groet
Ask for time	Eager to get on your schedule
Ask with gratitude	Thanks in advance for your help
Presumptive close	Looking forward to your reply
Objection handling	Can you let me know if you run into roadblocks? Thanks!
Lead to a LinkedIn invite	Look forward to connecting soon
Lead to a call	Speak with you soon
Lead to a chat	Looking forward to chatting
Lead to content	Hope the attached helps
Indicate follow-up to come	Stay tuned
Close/expect follow-up	That's all for now
Close releasing lead/insight	Happy to help if you like to learn more
Close releasing lead/convo	Let me know if you have any questions
Close with gratitude	Thanks again for_____
Close/short	Much appreciated!
Close funny	Typed on tiny keys, just for you.
Close early in the week	Have a great week
Close mid week	Hope your week is going well
Close late week	Have a great weekend (end of the week Thu/Fri)
Rejection w/o communication	Thank you for your consideration
Rejection with communication	Appreciate your time and consideration

STEP 5 Review! Test it

Review

- Review it with a peer – airmail it by saying it out loud.

- Do an A/B test to tune it and improve response rate.

EXERCISE: Identify the Rs in this email: Write out the full "R", then circle the good and bad below:

Hi Paul,

One of the career postings on your LinkedIn profile mentioned that your team at Acme is leveraging containers to help automate your deployments and development process.

We often see DevOps folks, much like yourself, having trouble achieving visibility, in real-time, into their siloed development tools. The inability to have full stack monitoring often slows the development cycle causing delays and errors in pushing out code.

{Customer}, for example, leveraged [my company] to help collect, centralize, and visualize their machine data in one place to proactively monitor deployments and gain full stack visibility.

Paul, do you think this could provide value to Acme?

Sarah

PS: This is an example you may like - check-out the 3rd paragraph.

2.4 Using Video in Emails

Instead of writing down long emails, leverage the power of video. Although video is a powerful visual aid, you should not use it like a SPAM email – make sure it is still relevant to your customer, and not just a pitch.

Here are a two proven situations showing when and how to use video as part of your outbound routine.

VIDEO EXAMPLE: **Use video as a hyper-personalized response**

Customer replies via email and asks you "how something works." Instead of explaining in email or screenshots, why not shoot an over-the-shoulder video. Have a colleague record you over your shoulder. Here is the script:

Figure 9: Use over-the-shoulder video to explain customer question

STEP 1 **[You looking over shoulder into camera with an intro] "Hi Mike - in follow-up to your question on _____ I wanted to show how to do this ..."**

STEP 2 **[Camera moves forward to capture your screen; you keep talking and pointing to direct the viewer's attention.]**

STEP 3 [Camera moves backward to capture you again, as you say] "Well Mike, hope that shows how easy this is. Let me know if you have more questions."

EMAIL EXAMPLE: Use of a cover email with a video to point challenges on their web-site

Mike - Noticed that you are passionate about customer satisfaction.

You seem to run into similar issues as <x> and <y>. I recently gathered insights from your website and created a short video for you. Here it is <LINK>, and check out the point being made at 1m 35secs.

Looking forward to hear from you – Jane

BEST PRACTICES

- **DO** use your customer's own material, such as website, download etc.

- **DO** open your dialogue, facing the camera, with the top problem.

- **DO NOT** introduce yourself, this gets taken care of in the cover email.

- **DO** Provide context: "What we see is that most people are experiencing these 3 problems...."

- **DO** visualize by drawing on a whiteboard.

- **DO NOT** pre-draw on a whiteboard – doesn't work.

- **DO** show how the issues all stem from the same problem, by drawing circles, arrows, etc.

- **DO** point out the solution and summarize how the solution can impact the key issues.

- **DO** NOT close formally and no need for a call to action – do that in the email.

- **DO** use your iPhone/tablet, etc. That HD/4K camera is good enough.

- **DO NOT** shake the camera too much – you'll get everyone dizzy!

- **DO** speak clearly - it's okay to use your headset microphone.

- **DO** shoot it in landscape mode, and position your face correctly (in the above example Kelly faces her screen correctly).

- **DO** keep it short: 30-45 seconds is great; > 60 seconds is too long.

- **DO** appear professional. A cool t-shirt is okay, but looking like you just rolled out of bed is **NOT.**

- **DO NOT** try to be perfect; a slight stutter, mishap, will all be okay. Think of it as if you are literally talking to the customer. You would not do a "let me start over" in a real conversation, right?

EXERCISE: **Create a video**

STEP 1 **This is a team exercise, so buddy up with a peer.**

STEP 2 **Pick a problem you hear a lot from a customer that you can resolve via a show-and-tell.**

STEP 3 **Have your buddy shoot a video of you demonstrating this (over your shoulder).**

BASIC SCRIPT

Opening: ....

Demo script:

First this: ....

Then this: ....

Then this: ....

Closing: ....

STEP 4 **Write a cover email (keep it short - half as long, twice as powerful)**

Cover email:

....

....

....

....

STEP 5 **Share it with your peers (who in turn may use it for their customers)**

2.5 Measure Engagement

For SDRs: Engage and Respond Immediately – Call them in < 5 minutes

- Respond within 5 minutes of the prospect watching the video! It has been shown time and time again that immediately reaching out by phone results in higher connect rates and great conversations.

- However, if you send them a 6-page use-case... you can't expect them to read it. With this, don't call them to ask if they read the article (clearly), but they probably would not read it anyway. You call them to give them the cliff notes and see what is important to them!!!

For AEs/CSMs: Get Executive Engagement – but it's on their time, not yours.

The best results come from immediate engagement. If a C-level executive responds on a Wednesday evening that he wants that white paper, and you send it the next day at 9 a.m., it will not get through his email clutter. HOWEVER, if you you send him that white paper 3-4 minutes after he requests it, there is a likelihood he forwards that paper immediately to the decision maker on the team!

This requires you to carefully plan your outbound schedules. If you have a campaign that goes out to 200 VPs of Sales at 9:56 a.m., you better block the next two hours for "immediate response." But also on a Sunday morning at 9 a.m. If you burden them with your email, you had better step up if they respond!

SDR/AE/CSMs Increasing Engagement

You need to monitor engagement: this means that you need to learn which factors will improve your open rates and click-through rates.

SDR/AE/CSMs Closing a Conversation

You should also understand the right time and the right way to end an email conversation.

Should it have a personalized signoff or a standard one? How do you reply to an answer of "no"? How should you send a reminder in a nice way? What's a good way to ask for feedback? Check out this post from Yesware (http://www.yesware.com/blog/how-to-end-an-email/) that runs through these key scenarios.

BEST PRACTICES

- DO keep it short. Shorter = better.

- DO NOT use bullets in your email – that will feel like marketing; instead be a bit more casual.

- DO NOT hide a link under a word. It makes it "suspicious," people like to know what they click on, and a link to a company domain is more trusted.

- DO test out short videos: We continue to see a high response rate to personalized videos. Test it.

- DO test windowing of your email. Response rates vary by time of day; schedule your outbound emails based on this knowledge:

  - Weekdays 9 p.m. (evening working exec).

  - Sunday at 9 a.m. (catching up/prep for the week).

  - Wednesday at 8 a.m. (generally best response rates).

  - Tue-Thu-Wed at 7 a.m. (mainstream window right before coffee).

3 Calling and Leaving a Voicemail

During outbound calling, it is normal for you to call a customer and leave a voicemail. Sounds simple enough, right? WRONG! Don't perform a voicemail off-the-cuff. Instead, you need to prepare for it and follow a framework to drive the best response rate possible. The 4 elements of a voicemail are:

- Preparing for leaving a voicemail.

- Dialing/navigating to get into voicemail.

- Leaving a voicemail.

- Following through with an email.

3.1 Preparing for a Voicemail

Give them something they see as valuable BEFORE you ask for them to attend a meeting with a specialist! This requires you to do two things:

STEP 1 **Perform basic research for the call (fill out the lines below based on a real customer):**

- Look up their corporate website...

- Do they have an active LinkedIn profile?...

- Look up their app/service/product. Free trial?...

- Do they have a 90 sec company YouTube video? ....

STEP 2 **Identify something of value to them that you can give:**

GIVE	WHAT IS IT?	WHY IS THIS VALUABLE TO THEM?
Use case	Find an example of a 3rd party that has a similar problem (same job title, industry or problem).	This helps them see who is doing what in the market, and how they can stay on top of new trends and best practices. The customer is selling, not you, which builds trust with your prospect.
Research data	Research or stats that they might find interesting in their role/function/industry.	Who doesn't love quick, snappy stats that can help them look smart in front of their boss?
White paper	An in-depth report on a specific topic.	White papers can provide some valuable perspective and save a lot of time for people who are looking for solutions, vendor evaluations, or simply looking to increase their knowledge in their industry.
Event	An industry or functional gathering for networking, training and knowledge enhancement.	Industry events are a great way for customers to network, increase their knowledge, and generate business. Find out what events are happening that they might be interested in, and you can even suggest that you meet at an event in person, if possible.

3.2 Dialing

Exactly how to make a call will be dependent on your company's phone server/system. We hope that you have this integrated into your CRM, so that all outbound call attempts are logged and all calls and voicemails are recorded.

PRO TIP When you want to get an executive on the phone, try calling the main company phone line around 6:10 p.m. The executive's EA has left at that time, and by navigating through the company's phone server, you can get to the executive's desk phone. The chances of the executive picking up at this time significantly increase with this approach.

– DAN SMITH

Navigating the customer's phone server

As you dial, you may hit the company's phone server. Below is an overview of a variety of servers and how to get to your customer by moving across the server (much needed in Account Based Marketing). Please take note that you WANT to hit the phone server. Essentially, you are able to circumvent many roadblocks and get straight to who you are looking for. Most phone servers only require the first three letters of the last name, enabling you to leave a personal message.

Some quick tips for navigating: Often the voicemail servers indicate which system they are. if not, try to hit *, #, or 0 in that order. You should be taken to some additional prompts, which will help you navigate the automated system. This can also be used to reach out to other people.

Phone Server	Operating Procedure
Audix	*8 to transfer by extension, #2 to transfer by name.
Avaya	To transfer to a mailbox, press 8, then follow the prompts to dial by name.
Cisco Unity	Hit * and it will tell you to *"Enter Your ID, Followed by #."* Just press # and it will take you back to the main menu. From there, most of the time it's 4 to get to the employee directory, but just listen to the prompts.
Inter-tel Axxess	Once you reach the voicemail box, press * and it will take you back to the auto attendant. Follow directory prompts from there.
Meridian Mail	You have two options: Either dial *70* or *7#, this should take you back to the auto attendant. If you get a message stating *"This person does not subscribe to this service,"* then hit the 1 key repeatedly and it will take you back to the extension or dial-by-name options.
Octel	This is a legacy system and the toughest to navigate. Pressing * or # will prompt you for a mailbox number to access your internal voicemail. However, many times, if you press 0 during the voicemail, you'll get an auto attendant.
Siemens HiPath Xpressions	If you try hitting * or # and you hear *"your input is not valid,"* then you're in an Xpressions system. Hit the 0 key during the voicemail, then listen to the prompts, but most of the time hitting * will get you to the dial-by-name directory.

3.3 Leaving a Voicemail

Voicemails are like email replies; you know only of the impact of when someone returns your call, not if they actually listened. So even though the average reply rate for voicemails is about 4 - 9%, you should still practice leaving great voicemails.

 **PRO TIP** Think of your voicemail as a hyper-personalized email personally delivered by you, with personality delivered through your voice.

- JACCO VAN DER KOOIJ

Your goal: NOT to get a call back. People hardly respond to calls these days. Instead, your primary objective is to draw attention to your email, and let them know you are valuable so that they give your email 10% extra attention.

BAD EXAMPLE: **Voicemail that will be deleted**

 Hello Mike - This is Jennifer from ACME. We offer a better way to do A B C with our X Y Z solution. We have customers such as APPLE and PEARS who are using us to get 10x return on their investment. I wanted to see if you are interested in chatting for 10 minutes. Please call me back at 123-456-7890.

The customer hits DELETE right after "APPLE" right? Here is Why:

- This sounds like a **cold call**.

- All about the vendor: **WE** offer, **WE** have, **I** wanted.

- Then you ask: I want 10 mins of your time.

GOOD EXAMPLE: Voicemail leading with relevance

Hi Esther - This is Mary from XYZ. First of all, thank you for connecting with me on LinkedIn <pause>

I notice that you have grown to a team of 8, and that you launched a new service on April 1. You must be in super-growth mode right now.

I wanted to offer you some insights gained from others similar to you. Please call me back at 123-456-7890. Again this is Mary from XYZ.

In this case, the customer hits delete right when you leave the phone number. Why this is better:

- Comes in as a **warm call**: Connection on LinkedIn.

- All about the customer: **YOU** have grown, **YOU** launched, **YOU** must be busy.

- Gives: ***Offers insights*** from your peers.

The key is that this must be delivered with high energy and passion in your voice!

GREAT EXAMPLE: Voicemail leading with relevance and including a call to action

Hi Esther - This is Mary from XYZ. First of all, thank you for connecting with me on LinkedIn <pause> I notice that you have grown to a team of 8, and that you launched a new service on April 1.

You must be in super-growth mode right now. I would like to offer you some insights gained from others in your situation, like ABC

Esther, I will send you an email to follow up, but feel free to call me at 123-456-7890 if that works better for you. Again this is Mary from XYZ.

What makes this call great?

- Use of the first name – draws Esther's full attention.
- You then deliver the call to action – "Look for my email."

EXERCISE: **Design your voicemail**

STEP 1 **Who are you:** ....

STEP 2 **Warm opening:** ....

....

STEP 3 **What is this about:** ....

....

STEP 4 **What is their reward:** ....

....

STEP 5 **Call to action:**   [Customer first name], I will follow up with an email, or if you prefer, you can reach me at ....

Again, this is .... from .... and my number is ....

3.4 Following Through

Be accountable - follow through when you say you will. Your customer may not always respond, but they will begin to recognize your polite persistence.

GREAT EXAMPLE: Follow-through message (no longer a cold email!).

Hi Preman - As promised in my voicemail please find below a link to ...

This should be relevant to you because...

4   Calling - The Conversation

In B2B, when a customer makes a decision, they may think about trade-offs that impact their job, their career, and potentially the future of their family. In comparison, in B2C, the impact of a decision is primarily transactional. A B2B buyer makes a commitment with long-standing implications, and they want to know not just **what** they are buying, but **who** they are buying from.

And your voice leaves an impression of who you are. Of course, they are not buying based on the sound of your voice alone. But hearing a calm voice can make ALL the difference in the world.

The most common use-case are:

- **Follow-up to any response/engagement from the customer:** for example, when a customer asks to learn more, our response is to call them.

- **Draw attention:** for example, by letting the customer know that you sent a proposal.

- **Outbound cold calls:** considered by most a nuisance but a cold call means you know nothing about the person you are calling and this is the first connection. To them, it sounds like this:

Hi Mary, I am someone you don't know. I really don't know anything about you,

Actually I don't even care, I just want to sell you something you probably will never use. Do you want to talk to me so I can waste 5 minutes of your life

and convince you to be harassed by a pesky sales person?

We are not saying you should minimize outbound calling! Absolutely not, phone calls are very powerful! What we are saying is that you should always try to make your phone call WARM, not

COLD. The trick is to get better information, to help you unpeel the onion faster. To accomplish this, you need to master the following elements of a phone call.

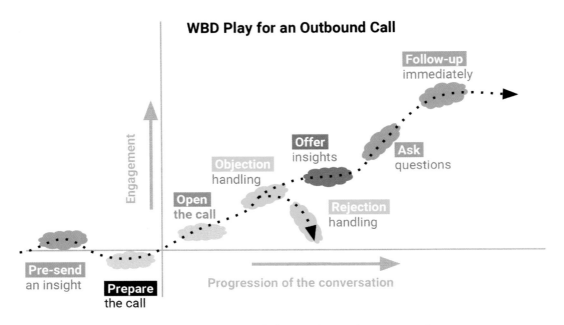

Figure 10: Framework for outbound conversation

4.1 Open – Creating Interest in Your First Sentence

The key to a great call is to have a great conversation. You cannot just start pitching. But the customer does want to know what the call is about. You have to be relevant to them. This means you must relate to their business situation.

The real COLD call is the preparation you did the day <u>before</u> the call, so the call you are making is actually *WARM*:

PRE-SEND an insight 1-2 days before the call.

PREPARE the call by doing your research: look up their LinkedIn profile, do a Google search on the company, and a quick Twitter visit on both the person and the company.

Empathy: What is client's problem: ....

How are you solving this: ....

Others with the same problem: ....

OPEN the call with an energetic tone addressing the 3 key questions the customer has:

- **Who are you:** Hi David, my name is _____ I work for ____
- **Why are you calling me:** The reason I am calling is _____
- **What's in it for me:** want to offer you a _____

GREAT EXAMPLE: **How to turn cold to warm ("+" indicates level of engagement)**

The Real Cold Call	Your "Warm" Call
Preparation you did the day before	Follow-up to the cold call
Visit their profile (+). They visit you back (++).	*Thank you for stopping by on my LinkedIn. I was wondering if...*
View (+), share (++) and/or comment (+++) on their blog post.	*Loved the recent post you published on... Have you looked at...*
Favorite a tweet (+) / Retweet (++).	*Your tweet yesterday was SPOT ON. It caught my attention and I was wondering...*

The Real Cold Call	Your "Warm" Call
Preparation you did the day before	Follow-up to the cold call
Pose a question on Quora (+); better yet post a response to their question (++).	*Great question on Quora. I thought would I pick up the phone and give you my answer...*
Send an email.	*Based on your background, I shared some insights earlier this week via email, and was wondering if you had time to take a look at it...*

WARM calling – the new approach to outbound sales calls

The key to using these levels of outbound sales calls to your advantage is to create what is called a WARM call.

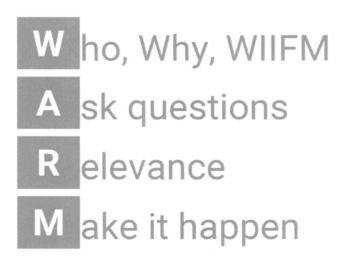

W ho, Why, WIIFM

A sk questions

R elevance

M ake it happen

W: Address the customer's confusion with three questions

The "W" in this acronym is all about addressing the customer's confusion. You do that by answering three important questions, that they are most likely thinking, as soon as possible on the call:

- Who are you?
- Why are you calling me?
- What's in it for me? (WIIFM)

A: Ask questions, instead of pitching

When you are making a warm outbound call, it's not the time to pitch about your product or service. Instead you want to be asking questions, and ask questions with context. The context proves that you've done your research.

For example, you may say something like "I noticed on LinkedIn that you are the Regional Vice President of Marketing at Acme Incorporated. Did I get that right?" Something as simple as this proves that you've done your research, and that the conversation is going to be relevant to that individual.

R: Establish relevance

You need to ensure that the ensuing questions are absolutely relevant to the prospect. These days there is no excuse for asking irrelevant or out-of-context questions. There is a wealth of information available online about: 1) the people that you're speaking to, 2) the company they work for, and 3) the industry that they are in. By researching these three elements, you're going to be able to identify certain facts that will enable you to be relevant in each of your conversations.

M: Make it happen for the customer

At this point, you are trying to provide some value to the person you are speaking to, ensuring that you are making their life easier. In the Regional Vice President of Marketing example, you may offer to provide some insight or information into how some of their competitors have entered certain markets or share a case study of how others have been successful, invite them to a webinar. You really need to think about what is important and will add value for them and invite them to engage with you further.

4.2 Objections

The top OBJECTIONS are:

- Who is this again? (Tonation makes the difference between an objection or rejection.)

- Email me!

- Not now, I am busy!

- I am the wrong person!

These objections apply to SDRs during outbound, but also to AEs and CSMs as they navigate through an organization.

In order to increase your success rate, you need to:

- **Develop** a proper response to all of these objections.

- **Practice** it before you make calls.

- **Print** it and hang it on your monitor.

The key to objection handling is to give them something more that they do want, to prevent them from moving on with their day and getting you off the phone. This means you have to offer them something.

Objection: **Not now:** Can you call me back next month?

Initial value: Get you off the phone.

Real value: Get their own name out of your CRM.

This is not a good time. Can you call me back next month?

Mike, you don't want me to call you back next month if I am not relevant to you. I would rather scratch you you off the list so I don't bother you any longer - make sense?

OK. What is this about?

The reason I am calling is... relevance... relevance... relevance..

Relevance: You must be relevant in a few ways:

- Relevance 1: I know who you are and what you do.
- Relevance 2: I suspect you have a problem with this.
- Relevance 3: Because I noticed this and this...

EXAMPLE: **Not me**

Objection: **Not me** : I am not the right person.

Initial value: Deflect your call.

Real value: Don't really know if this is relevant; wants to cover their behind.

BAD EXAMPLE: Most common response that dead-ends:

I am not the right person.

Who is the right person?

Why don't you send me an email - I will forward it on!

GOOD EXAMPLE: Instead consider this approach:

I am not the right person.

May I ask for a quick favor.

I have been looking around to learn more about your company/offering...

besides your website do you know a good place where I can find more info?

Have you tried our blog?

Let me look... yes that's exactly what I am looking for.

Did you write any of the posts?

I did not.

I am sure you will soon enough.

<first name> after I complete my research who should I ask for?

You see how you are leading with knowledge and how this suddenly becomes customer-centric?

Objection:	**Email me your material and I will take a look**
Initial value:	I am possibly interested and I want to be polite to you
Real value:	They can't say no -- they may tell their boss they looked at your company

Consider this approach

... Can you email me more information?

Sure what would you like me to send you?

Send me an outline of _____.

Great! I am going to prepare a custom outline for you right now!

May I ask what your current infrastructure is so that I can make it relevant?

... ask question #2..

...ask question #3..

... Thank you so much!

You see how you are leading with knowledge, and how this suddenly becomes customer-centric?

BEST PRACTICES

- **DO** your research and be relevant to them!

- **DO NOT** reflexively say right after they spit out an objection "I understand." No, you don't understand. You did extensive research, and this person has a problem you can help with.

- **DO NOT** ask a question to which the answer is a negative: "Do you have a few moments?"

- **DO NOT** start with negative/apology "I am so sorry to bother you, the reason I am calling..."

- **DO NOT** agree to follow up when they ask. "Sure I will get back to you" then wait to follow-up 2-3 months without doing anything. You think that you are properly following up at their request. Guess what? Your customers don't set reminders that "Johnny is going to follow up," so they see you as a digital stalker when you call them 2 months later.

EXERCISE: **Objection handling**

- Get a group of 3-5 of you together; this should include AEs, CSMs, marketing, etc.

- Establish the 4 key objections.

- Role play how each objection would go.

- Round-robin the objection until you feel confident you have a plan:

Objection: ....

Response: ....

....

Pre-strike/Research: ....

Do this for all key objections!

4.3 Rejections

The most common REJECTIONS **are:**

- Who is this again? (Tonation makes the difference between an objection or rejection.)
- I am not interested.
- Take me off your list.

EXAMPLE: I am not interested

Initial value: I am just not into you and I want to be polite to you.

Real value: Get you off the phone and out of my life.

Consider this:

Sorry - I am not interested.

The reason I called you was ... and ... but if you say my research was wrong I'll gladly move on

Really not interested!

Got it. <our company> is not for everyone.
Thank you for your patience.

EXAMPLE: Take me off your list

Initial value: I don't know you.

Real value: You don't know me. I don't trust you. I am fed up with these calls bothering me.

Consider this:

Please take me off your list..

                               Absolutely. Mike may I provide you my number...

Sorry? What? Why?

                             Sometimes these system have a hard time getting people out of the system and I want you to have a person you can call.
Just in case it is not working as intended.

That's appreciated.

BEST PRACTICES

- **DO** stay empathetic – this person has been called dozens of times.
- **DO NOT** get emotionally involved.
- **DO NOT** push – today one bad client on Twitter can wreak havoc.
- **DO** represent your company.

4.4 Offer Something of Value

A few things we can give that are valuable are:

- Invite to speak with others.

- Invite to listen in on a webinar.

- Meet with an expert to review their situation.

- Demonstration to visualize how we can help.

- Setup a trial to test it out.

EXAMPLE: Giving/offering something that they perceive to be of value

Honestly I run into this all the time. If you like, I can set you up with an expert who can review your situation.

Hmmm.. is this going to be a 30-minute demo?

Well that depends?

Depends on what?

We can certainly do a 30-min demo, but we've found if we put your data into the demo it will be a lot more useful for you.

I can see that.

Is this urgent? In which case, we can see if we have an opening this afternoon, or if not, we can do it tomorrow. Your call?

Let's do this afternoon.
I need to get this on my plate.

4.5 Ask Questions

GOOD EXAMPLE: Asking questions using situational and pain questions in an ideal scenario

How many employees do you have that submit expense reports every week?

We have 12 people.

Which tools do they use today?

They use Excel spreadsheets.

Do you have challenges with timely filing of reports?

The team often files them with finance on the last day of the month - our busiest time!

How does that impact your business?

*The finance team works overtime, causing lots of **frustration**.*

Although this is a good example, it is hard to get the customer into a discussion like this. They are not surrendering these details. So you have to pre-empt them with insights gained and open/closed question sequences.

GREAT EXAMPLE: Asking questions using open/closed to create an ideal scenario

*I notice on LinkedIn you have 12 people
On your team; do I get that right?*

Yes, although we added 2 more.

*Most companies your size seem to work with Excel.
What tools do you use?*

Same here - we also use Excel.

*Do you have challenges
with timely filing of reports?*

Yes.

What are the ones that worry you the most?

*The team files expense report on the
last day of the month - our busiest time!*

How does that impact your business?

*The finance team has to work overtime,
causing lots of **frustration**.*

In this case, we are identifying:

- **CRITICAL EVENT:** Every month they go through this; end of year probably even more. But also new hires, sales kickoffs are all events that create a moment in time to fix this once and for all.

- **IMPACT:**

  - Emotional: Frustration, often leading to people complaining or worse resigning.

  - Rational: Overtime cost, issues in reporting due to time constraints etc.

4.6 Follow-up - Next Steps

GREAT EXAMPLE: **Follow-through message (no longer a cold email).**

Ollie,

Thank you for today's call. To summarize: you have 14 employees, most of whom are working remotely. They submit their expense report using Excel, often on the last day of the month when your finance is extremely busy. This is causing a headache and loss of revenue. Did I get that right?

I have cc'd our resident expert Jennifer – today at 2 p.m. she will be able to diagnose your situation, demo how to resolve, and provide some best practices.

For your convenience, I sent a calendar invite with screen share and dial-in information. Don't hesitate to let me know if I missed anything.

Christina

5   Socializing

In the conventional sales world, it was all about the one decision maker. Now, decisions are made as a team. There are several stakeholders at play, so it is important to understand their priorities are in line with the prescription you have helped define.

The reason why 'socializing' in selling is so important is:

- It takes place from the "O'SH!T" moment all the way through to the "AHA" moment (see below); this is the most complicated part of the entire sales cycle (normally covered with cold calling).

- The efforts scale 24/7.

- It is a form of asynchronous selling, where a seller and a buyer operate at a different speed.

- Most of it is performed in written/visual communication, allowing for easy preparation/scaling.

 **PRO TIP** Over the past year, we have seen a declining trend in use of LinkedIn as a targeting tool. We strongly discourage the use of LinkedIn and other social tools to engage in "cold outbound" or worse "sales pitch." Best way to use LinkedIn is to sincerely build a network of similarly minded professionals with whom you are sharing best practices.

– DOMINIQUE LEVIN

5.1 Visiting Customers Online

Find the right people at the company. Click through 10+ profiles in your target company, and every day make sure you visit 100+ profiles of prospective customers.

EXAMPLE: LinkedIn helps you with surfing profiles

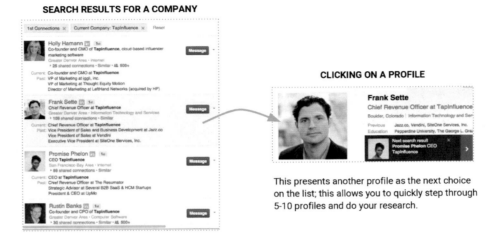

BEST PRACTICES Social selling technique

- Use a saved search list.

- Visit all the profiles in the saved list.

- View "who's viewed your profile" at least once a day to see who visits you back.

- If they visit back, reach out **BUT only if you have your LinkedIn profile prepared.**

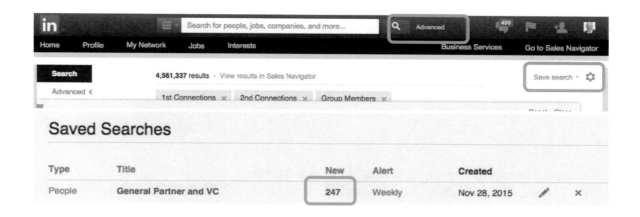

Figure 11: LinkedIn Saved Search highlighting new leads

EXAMPLE: Outbound LinkedIn message (no longer an Inmail!)

 Thank you for visiting! Were any of the insights I provided of value to you? Your profile says you work on x and y - that makes me think <u>this article</u> may be of use to you.

5.2 Listening to Customers Online

Start to learn what your market is talking about by listening, understanding how they talk, what industry lingo they use, etc.

Use tools to push information to you every day. It would take too much time to always search for each customer, news source, social network and recheck throughout the day. Therefore, set up tools that help follow things directly.

STEP 1 **Which of your customers are active?**

Twitter Accounts   Topics they talk about

@ ....   # ....

@ ....   # ....

@ ....   # ....

STEP 2 **Who are the top industry "insiders"? Follow them!**
Create lists by topic, industry, etc. on TweetDeck

Twitter Accounts   LinkedIn INfluencers

@ ....

@ ....

@ ....

STEP 3 **What are the industry trends #problem-abc, and the events #events-xyz?**

@ ....   # ....

@ ....   # ....

@ ....   # ....

QUORA EXAMPLE: Guy Nirpaz, CEO and founder of Totango, listens to this conversation on Quora. The public article allows him to engage, and as he responds, he creates NEW content. That content performs as a Lead Generation for months to years.

5.3 Engaging with Customers Online

There are two kinds of engagement:

- **Passive**: Likes, Nudges, etc.

- **Active**: Directly mentioning, referring or addressing your customer.

See the following two pages for examples of these types of engagement.

PASSIVE ENGAGEMENT

Passive engagements are very non-intrusive and can be considered an outbound "call." These nudges are a great tool for an AE to expand a network within an existing account, or to re-energize a relationship that has "gone dark."

Type of Engagement	What Is It?	What Does It Look Like
LINKEDIN EXAMPLE The non-message touch	• **Following:** You stay up to speed on your customer and what they are doing, while the customer sees you are following them, that you care. • **Commenting:** In case your customer shares a post, your customer will be notified on the comments on that post. If your comments are insightful, this leaves an "expert" impression. • **Endorsing:** Be careful with this, but a person you have been having meetings with appreciates if you provide a positive engagement. • **Re-sharing:** People love views, re-shares and likes on their articles. • **Liking:** A very gentle nudge, but often seen and appreciated.	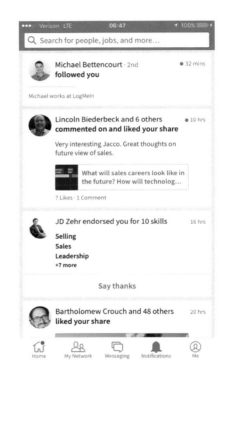

Type of Engagement	What Is It?	What Does It Look Like
TWITTER **EXAMPLE** 140 characters + actions	• Fewer people are on Twitter these days, but for some customer bases, this still may be very relevant. • **Follow:** You stay up to speed on your customer and what they are doing, while the customer sees you are following them, that you care. • **Mention:** In case your customer shares a tweet. • **Retweet:** Retweeting with a mention of the customer has high visibility. • **Love:** Very gentle nudge, but high visibility and appreciated.	

ACTIVE ENGAGEMENT

Type Of Engagement	What Is It?
LINKEDIN **EXAMPLE** Message types	• **Connection Request - Always customize:** In the U.S., this can happen after a phone outreach; in Europe and Asia, this can only happen after you have established a relationship. • **InMail - Similar to RRRR:** Part of emailing when cold, and part of texting when a connection. But be careful about the type of relationship that you have with the person!
TWITTER **EXAMPLE**	• **Direct Message:** Part of social selling; be careful!

BEST PRACTICES

- DO contribute a comment using your personal insights.

- DO provide real insights to help your customer.

- DO NOT sell your services in response to any conversation UNLESS specifically asked to do so.

- DO make comments – relate to how other customers made a decision. Think of PARLA:

  - What Problem did they experience.

  - What Action did they take.

  - What Result did they get out of this.

  - What did they *Learn* from it.

  - How did they *Apply* this moving forward.

  - But...DO NOT mention your product/service.

GREAT EXAMPLE: Dan Smith shows how it's done...

Shawn Hickman 2nd
Inside Sales Strategist

I have read many of these and believe Predictable Revenue is the best of those i've read. I'm often asked what book a sales person should read and my first response is always Dale Carnegie's How to Win Friends and Influence People. The book is nearly 80 years old and I read it the first time nearly 20 years ago. It's as relevant today as it was when it was written.

Like · Reply(1) · 3 months ago

Dan Smith AUTHOR 1st
Helping SaaS companies scale sales

Great point - yes Carnegies book is awesome. Did you see Vorsights post on the 5 problems with Predictable Revenue? Although I love Aarons book, this is an interesting breakdown of where it falls short: http://vorsightbp.com/blog/5-problems-with-predictable-revenue-by-aaron-ross/

Like · 3 months ago

6   Messaging

Messaging is a short-form, instant, real-time communication that has been growing in popularity as people start to become burdened with too many emails.

- **Short form:** use of minimal amount of words or even abbreviations.

- **Instant**: have the conversation when the customer wants it (need pricing now).

- **Real-time**: Back and forth separated by seconds.

Services like SMS and Twitter have been based on this short-form communication for a while, but now other services such as Intercom, Slack and Zendesk are using messaging as a way to communicate with customers in a B2B setting. Below is an overview of some of the tools (not meant to be an exhaustive list):

An overview of messaging tools used in today's communication:

Intercom	LinkedIn	Twitter
Text Message	WhatsApp	Zendesk
Slack	LiveChat	Google Chat

Different tools - different audiences

Although all of these are designed to be used in real time, they have a distinct difference in terms of how they are used. For example, Intercom and Zendesk are "real-time," meaning that they are used as live chat on a website where immediate action is required. With LinkedIn, texting, and WhatsApp, the message is always present, regardless if you log in the next day. And in applications like Slack and Twitter, an older message will be snowed under in sheer volume of more recent messages, and has a high chance of becoming irrelevant the next day.

6.1 Messaging Basics

The latest way customers prefer to buy is through short and to-the-point communication. Long emails are never fully read, and rarely get the desired response. Just remember:

GREAT EXAMPLE: **Keep it short!**

How Not To Do It	How To Do It
→ The most common mistake: when people use the same style of short form texting in an email.	→ Used for quick back and forth, thus ultra short and action-driven.

How Not To Do It

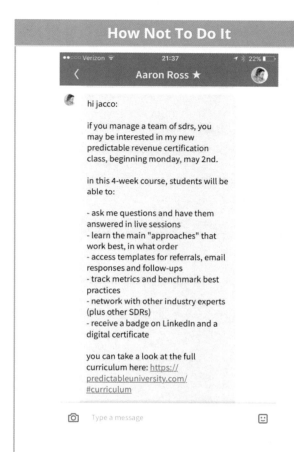

How To Do It

Key areas of improvement:

→ One-way message rather than conversational.

→ Too long.

→ Not personalized enough.

→ Uses bullets (looks like a marketing email).

→ All I, Me, Us.

Key areas of improvement:

→ Took too long for me to respond.

→ Rapid back and forth, but still too slow.

→ Short and to the point, but can be even shorter.

→ Make the action even more specific.

→ Lack of use of emoticons to personalize.

6.2 Real-time Messaging

More and more, we will see real-time messaging playing a vital role in Sales Development, Sales and Customer Success. What is real-time messaging? When a customer visits your web property, such as your website home page, you have a unique opportunity to start a conversation.

GOOD EXAMPLE: Online SDR using the chat box to secure a meeting

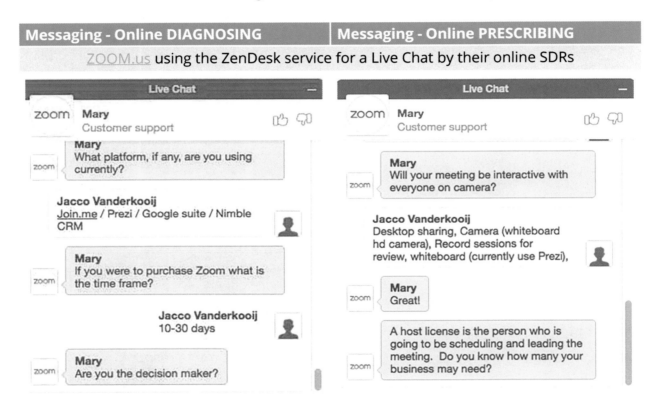

Key areas of improvement:

- Mary is mixing diagnosing and prescribing. Here she should be sticking with questions like:

    - Why am I moving away from my existing platform?

    - Is there specific use-case I am looking for?

    - Is there a sense of urgency to have the problem resolved?

But also:

- Mary is a logo, she should put up a picture of her face to humanize her.

- Excellent use of short back and forth.

- Lacks use of emoticons and punctuation to personalize.

Key areas of improvement:

Once Mary has diagnosed, she should have moved to prescribing the best solution for me:

1. Diagnose the customer's problem, not qualify the customer to "sell to."

2. Recommend a solution based on customer needs (not your own criteria).

3. Ask customer if you got it right?

4. Ask to move forward to a meeting with a specialist, not a person who sells to you.

A closer look

At first glance you may say… what is so special about this? But taking a closer look, you will notice the following:

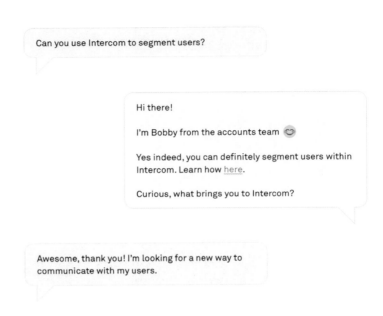

- Bobby introduced himself.
- Humanized himself with an emoji.
- Gave the answer immediately.
- Provided value with a link.
- Then asked a diagnostic question.

What a great start of a conversation!!! Compare this to the earlier conversation (interrogation) with Zoom and you will notice the difference.

Training and preparation

Success like this is not a coincidence, but the outcome of training and preparation:

- Establish a list of diagnostic questions.
- Study your use-cases.
- Create a list of resources to share instantly with "why" and "where to find it."
- Qualification questions (please absolutely NO use of BANT!).
- Memorize shortcuts of the 10 best emoticons that are appropriate for your conversations.

A good article that describes some best practices was captured by Bobby at Intercom.io, and can be found here: "Finding the clues in real-time sales messaging". In general, it's important to mirror your writing style and tone with that of your customers.

BEST PRACTICES

DO set expectation with greetings.

- Do they introduce themselves? If so, with a full name or on a first-name basis?

- Do they list additional contact info? A company name or job title?

- An insistence on job titles can be a sign that someone works at a bigger or well established company where communication will be more formal and buying cycles will be longer.

DO use the right lexicon.

- You want your response to be understood above all, so it's best to err on the side of clarity when it comes to word choice.

- Visitor dives head-first into technical terms? Match that style.

- Nerds love fellow nerds! Don't be a afraid to be a nerd.

DO mirror the writing style (formal, essay or email).

- This is a good sign that you can go into a bit more detail.

- Time is probably less urgent in these situations.

- It's a good idea to avoid SMS abbreviations, emoji and other chat-speak, as it might not be fully understood.

- Offer proactive information in addition to answering any questions.

DO mirror if the user writes in show burst, abbreviated vocabulary etc.

- These customers might be a bit more inclined to chat-based shorthand, and perhaps more familiar with the messaging format in general.

- Speed and urgency are crucial.

DO use emoticons.

- Smiley faces provide a great opening - who doesn't want to talk to a friendly person?

- A rocket ship can represent growth and progress, usually important in B2B conversations ;-)

- A thumbs up is perfect for agreement or confirming your solutions.

- A speech bubble is a great way to leave things open for further questions.

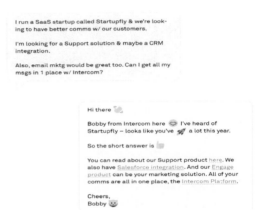

DO it in the right order

- **Answer their question** first – they reached out to ask you something, so make sure you 'give to get!'

- **Introduce yourself** – no one ever was kicked to the curb for having manners.

- **Establish rapport**, show that you care! No, seriously – show that you REALLY care!

- **Diagnose** their situation first – do not multitask here, stay focused. Remember prescription before diagnosis is malpractice!

- Then (and this is important) **Provide Value** to them – a link, an online resource, etc. Highlight why you provided that link, and where they can find what.

- Then and only then, **Prescribe** a solution – preferably without mentioning your service too overtly (that's why they contacted you in the first place!).

7 Setting Up a Meeting

Every customer-facing professional knows that forward progress is made primarily through meetings and calls. These meetings can be for discovery, performing a demo, discussing a proposal, onboarding, training, etc. Every meeting should consist of these elements:

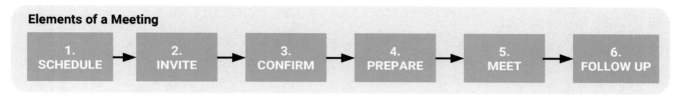

This seems straightforward, but the basic hygiene of managing meeting flow is absolutely crucial to a great customer experience.

7.1 Scheduling the Online Meeting

Scheduling of a discovery call/meeting needs to be done quickly; otherwise, the customer loses their interest. If you use a scheduling program, make sure that you word the invitation correctly, for example:

BAD EXAMPLE: **Do not transfer responsibility to the customer**

Please click on my schedule to book a date that works for both of us:

<LINK TO ONLINE SCHEDULER>

Although this sounds good, it actually is not as good as you think. Why?

- You are asking the customer to do work that you were supposed to do.

- It feels like the customer's schedule is secondary to your schedule.

GOOD EXAMPLE: Make it more customer-centric

 To find a match with your schedule across different time zones, please book a date that is most convenient for you: <LINK TO ONLINE SCHEDULER>

As you can see, customer-centric selling is not just a tagline; it finds its way into everything that you do.

7.2 Inviting People to the Online Meeting

A quality invitation creates brand awareness

To get something accomplished, you have to talk to the right people! A sales professional is able to get the right people in the room at the right time. This means (s)he gets better answers to questions, makes more progress, and earns the business at a higher level. This does not happen by accident, but is the outcome of a tried-and tested-system.

EXAMPLE: How an invitation travels through a company

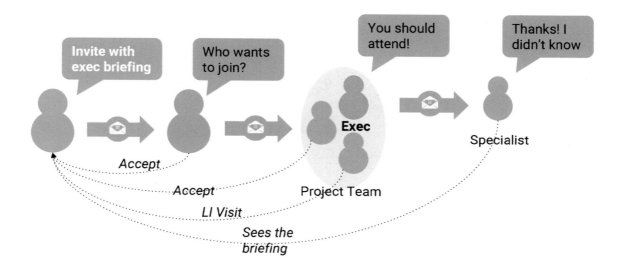

Figure 12: Sending an executive briefing can circulate within your customer's company

1. You send out a professional invite to the prospect.

2. Your customer accepts the invite and forwards it to several team members, inviting them to join.

3. Team members accept the invite, giving you insight into who is on the team.

4. One of the team members visits your LinkedIn profile, you connect with them and send an inquiry.

5. The executive involved scans over the invite, and realizes that a specialist needs to be involved.

6. The specialist, invited by the executive, clicks on the research (value) you included.

Your invite just created awareness, while benefiting your customer (value!).

CHECKLIST

☐ **Goal of the meeting:** Problem/Vision – A description of what you want to get done.

☐ **Value**: A link to an article that provides more details, such as your vision.

☐ **Who**: Names with hyperlinks to LinkedIn profile – easy for them to click on.

☐ **When**: Meeting date, time and time zone.

☐ **How**: Make it clear which number to dial.

☐ **Where**: Screenshare information (such as join.me).

☐ Mobile contact information.

Ask yourself... will this really make a difference for every meeting? Yes, it will. Make it count.

BEST PRACTICES

- DO clearly identify the dial-in number, top of the invite, single click dial capability.

- DO include your personal direct number they can dial in case of any issues.

- DO NOT attach any materials – include hyperlinks instead.

- DO NOT make it a book – it needs to print on one page (one side).

EXAMPLE: Initial meeting invitation

Goal: To do a show-and-tell the service and how it meets your requirements, to give your team the real UI/UX experience, and to show the integration with your CRM.

Click to join:

+42 408-123 4567,,765432

https://join.me/yournamehere

When: *Tuesday 2 pm EST (local time)*

Invited:

John D (Link to LinkedIn profile)
Mary Smith (Link to LinkedIn profile)

Agenda:

- *Requirements review*

- *Show and tell (vs. requirements)*

- *Address any open issues*

Learn more:

- *Link to an article with insights (Whiteboard Prezi that shows ins/outs)*

- *Link to a video with insights (Customer X implementation and lessons learned)*

In case of questions, feel free to call me at 123-456-7890

7.3 Preparing for the Online Meeting

Similar to preparing an email... If you know more about the customer, the impact of their imminent decision – and you have the right solution – you will win! This power is earned by thorough online research, which signals to your customer that you care about them. And the information you desperately seek is often laying around in plain sight.

As you prepare for the meeting, identify your ideal outcome of the call.

If you're looking to determine an understanding of how they would bring on your solution, write down the questions you will ask to get that understanding.

Write down the name of everyone who will be attending the meeting, and do 2-3 minutes of research on each attendee before the call.

CHECKLIST

Industry-Specific	Company-Specific
☐ Finance	☐ Crunchbase
☐ Ad Tech	☐ TechCrunch
☐ Software	☐ LinkedIn (size, goal)
☐	☐ YouTube Overview Video
☐	☐ ....
☐	☐ ....

Problem-Specific	Person-Specific
☐ Google/YouTube	☐ Twitter
☐ SlideShare	☐ Facebook
☐ Company website	☐ LinkedIn profile
☐ Subscribe to their service	☐ Google Images (search for their name)
☐ Submit a "bug"	☐ ....
☐	☐ ....
☐	☐ ....

A modern sales professional, armed with an iPad and WiFi connectivity, will be able to track digital footprints and get a basic understanding of what is going on with the account/opportunity.

7.4 Confirming the Online Meeting

CONFIRMATION #1: The call before the call

If there are multiple people on the call, the Development Rep (SDR) MUST inform the Account Exec/Sales Manager (AE) so that the AE can place a separate phone call BEFORE the online meeting takes place.

This call takes place with your champion. In this call, the AE has to ask for the champion's guidance on the meeting, any insights you need to know, and the roles and goals of the other attendees. Your outbound email to request this call can be short and to the point, something like:

 Mike, looking forward to our meeting scheduled for Friday. I noticed several people are attending. Can we talk today between 3-5pm? I want to make sure we accomplish your goals.

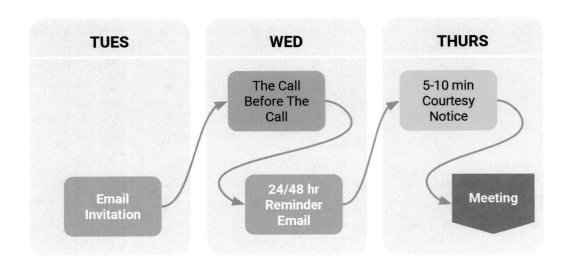

Figure 13: When to send reminders for scheduled meetings

CONFIRMATION #2: 24/48 hour reminder

24 hours before the meeting, you need to send a helpful/kind reminder to the attendee:

We are very much looking forward to seeing you this Thursday at 10am PST. Please find below a recently published article that outlines issues very similar to the ones you are encountering, and what actions the company took.

http://link to article - with expert advice from a respectable source

If anything comes up, please do not hesitate to reach out to me. I am here to help!

- **DO** include a copy of the invite/agenda in the confirmation email below the body of your message. The key of this reminder is to make sure they attend. BUT this also this gives them the opportunity to forward the meeting and invite more people.

- **DO** include links to relevant articles. By including a relevant article for them to read, you once again create value-add in the sales process. You can open the call by asking who read the article, and asking them their take on it. This gives you an opportunity to let them "sell" your points based on the article you provided them (a customer use-case?).

CONFIRMATION #3: **5-minute courtesy email**

5-10 minutes before the call, the Development Rep or AE needs to send out a courtesy message:

PRO TIP Include commas to automatically add in meeting ID
For example: Instead of having them "dial (415) 123-4567, then enter meeting ID: 999-888-777 followed by #" - Instead include one-click dial-in from your phone: 4151234567,,9998887777

- DAN SMITH

Courtesy message for all attendees:

Single click dial-in: xxx.xxx.xxxx,,123456789

Link: www.personalized.com/heretohelpyou

If anything comes up, do not hesitate to reach out on my cell at 123.456.7890

7.5 Opening and Running the Online Meeting

Have you ever had a great discovery call, but right as you were about to set up next steps, the customer has to abruptly leave the meeting? Then you're left chasing them down, or the deal completely fades and eventually is lost. Or even worse, you get on a call and halfway through, you realize the customer wanted a full-on technical demo but you were only prepared to discuss how to set up a pilot. Yikes!

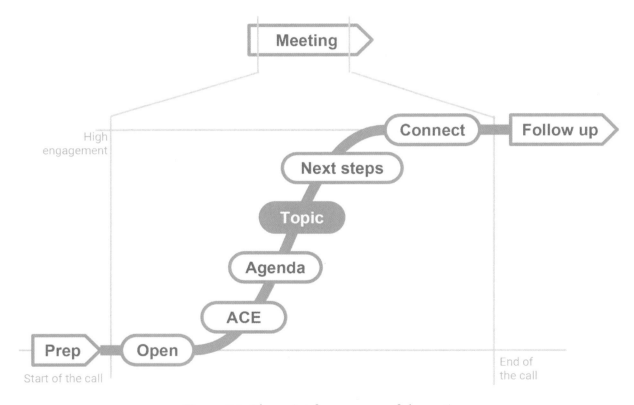

Figure 14: Blueprint for a successful meeting

STEP 1 **Prepare for the meeting**

Goal: Be ready. Be relevant to the customer.

Send out courtesy email with the details, set up your browser tabs, make sure the technology works! Perform your last-minute research, and be on the call 1-2 minutes before the call starts.

STEP 2 **Open the conversation**

Goal: Set yourself up as a friendly professional.

Inquire what is going on in their world. Ask who will be joining the call. This is also a good time to mention (and ask for approval) that you will be taking notes and recording the call. What you should NOT do is start political, sports debates or worse how great the weather is where you are. Keep it short!

STEP 3 **Perform an ACE to open the call**

Goal: Structure the meeting using ACE – this shows the customer that:

1. You're a prepared, thoughtful and professional.
2. This is a 2-way conversation, not a 1-sided demo.
3. You want to make it relevant and efficient for both parties.

Outline of an ACE opening:

A – Appreciate	***Appreciate** you joining our call today*
C – Confirm end time	*We are **scheduled until** the bottom of the hour, does that work?*
E – End Goal	*The end goal of this call concludes with {X or Y}.*
	Does that sound like a good use of our time today?

This should take no more than 45-60 seconds, and make sure you ask and confirm their timing for the meeting. If they only have 5 minutes, maybe you should reschedule. For the first 20 times you start a scheduled call, use these exact words – then once you're comfortable, you can change them to something more natural for you.

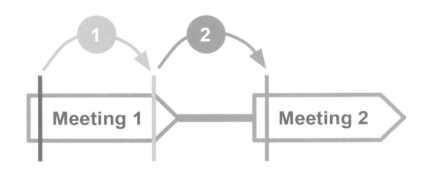

Figure 15: Connecting the end goal of the call to next meeting

The magic of ACE is that you set yourself up for success:

- Confirmed the end-time – in particular with the decision maker.

- Set a goal for the end of the meeting (see 1) so you get to the decision you set forth to do (see 2).

We just have a few minutes left; have we accomplished the goal you had for this call?

Yes, we did.

As we discussed at the beginning of the call,

are you ready to move forward with _____?

That depends on Mary – Mary, what do you think?

STEP 4 **Set the agenda**

Goal: Establish what they want to discuss … and much more.

You now need to confirm the agenda, by asking each person in the meeting what they are looking to get out of today's meeting. Make sure you write it down, and make sure that you address each and every one on the call. If there are more than 4 people on the call, we recommend you do this with your champion as outlined in the call-before-the-call. You then summarize what your champion has told you and ask the group as a whole if they want to add anything.

May I ask: what do you want to accomplish on this call?

I want to learn about how the platform
works and get an idea if it can help me with XYZ problem.

Okay. So you want to learn about how to address your
problem and how our platform works. Anything else?

Yes and get an idea of your price.

Yes we can tackle that too. Mike, did you want to add anything?

I'd love to learn more about your global support.

Got it!

Then obtain a first glimpse into the decision criteria:

That's a lot to talk about in the allotted time. May I ask what is the most
pressing issue?

How the product works and how it
can help me solve XYZ problem.

Okay – why don't we start with those two topics
And address the others at the end?

Sounds like a plan.

STEP 5 Perform the topic of the call/meeting

Goal: Deliver the value for which the call/meeting was scheduled.

At this point, you perform the topic of the call; this commonly is one of the following:

- Discovery call to diagnose the problem a client is experiencing.

- Demonstration to present a solution or a vision of a better tomorrow.

- A combined Disco/Demo where your service is used to deepen a discovery.

- Proposal review call to discuss the details of your offer.

- Price/Terms negotiation to come to a mutual agreement.

- Kick-off call to go over the roll-out of the service.

- Etcetera.

More details on this can be found in Chapter 6 where several examples are provided.

STEP 6 Agree to next steps

Goal: Establish what they want to discuss.

This is one of the most critical moments in the call – this moment needs to occur about 5 minutes before the decision maker leaves the call. The key is to link this back to the "E" in ACE; once we've established that we've achieved what the call was set up for, we now follow up with what the goal of the call was.

Mary and Mark being conscious of your time ... May I ask was I able to address your questions you had at the beginning of the call?

Yes, you did thank you.

I ask because, at the beginning of the call, we discussed the next step being a meeting to review our proposal.

Are you ready to move forward with that?

I am – Mary are you okay with that as well?

STEP 7 **Connecting the meetings**

Goal: Orchestrate the success of the next call right now. Assist them to use the entire experience.

Here's what happens if we **DO NOT** do that right:

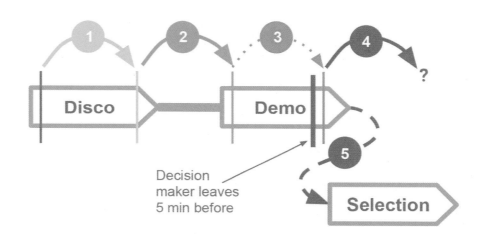

Figure 16: The importance of defining end goals across multiple meetings

To recap, we are using **ACE** to set up the goal of the meeting (see 1). At the end of the meeting, we then agree to move forward based on the goal (see 2). However, on the next call, we forget to do the **ACE** (see 3). Then the decision maker who was on the call leaves 5 minutes early. Your sponsor cannot agree to the follow-up without talking to the team, e.g. the decision maker who just departed (see 4). They tell you that they will get back to you – and the deal goes dark (see 5).

We do not want this to happen – we must connect the meetings so that there is a smooth flow between all touchpoints, and we can continue to move the deal along.

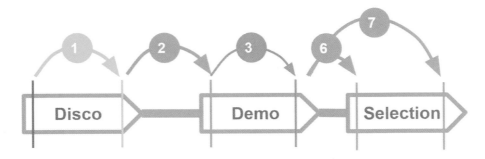

Figure 17: Re-apply the end goal to connect the wagons

Now by re-applying ACE, we reconnect the meeting but it also allows us to do this. With the decision maker in the room, we agree that we addressed the questions and we agree to a follow-up meeting (see 6). We can then ask...

What would you like to get out of the next meeting?

Which in turn allows us to ask...

Who are the best people we can get into the meeting to accomplish that goal?

That allows us to orchestrate the end of the next meeting (see 7) and with it we start to assist the client through the buying process.

7.7 Follow up After the Meeting

Following up after the meeting is critically important, as it secures the progress you just made. You write the summary, not aimed AT your champion, but FOR your champion. When you create a proper summary, and do it shortly after the call, your customer will likely copy and paste a large part of your summary into their internal briefing. Customer-centric superstars see and use this as an opportunity.

CHECKLIST

☐ Outline the key observations and accomplishments.

☐ Outline the action items and next steps.

BEST PRACTICES

- **DO** contact your champion and verify! Right after the meeting (seconds to minutes), call your champion and ask him/her if (s)he is happy with what was accomplished. Verify your takeaways!

- **DO** block several minutes post-meeting to do your follow-up.

- **DO** make your follow-up short and to the point.

- **DO** separate your follow-up into two parts (but in 1 email).

- **DO** write meeting minutes, with the intent to brief others who were NOT on the call; better yet, share the notes you took in the shared doc. Quick/fast!

- **DO** effectively use the subject line – consider it as your 60 character result summary/follow-up.

- **DO** write it in such a way that it can easily be shared.

7.8 Presenting in Real Time (TAB-based Presenting)

Customers are expecting a great sales experience and are frustrated with the standard way of sharing features. One of the best ways to stay engaging is kind of like sharing the journey you will be going on by showing them each chapter of the demo.

Below is a picture of real-time selling, (AKA tab-based selling). A browser pre-loaded with content is used to guide a customer through the discovery call.

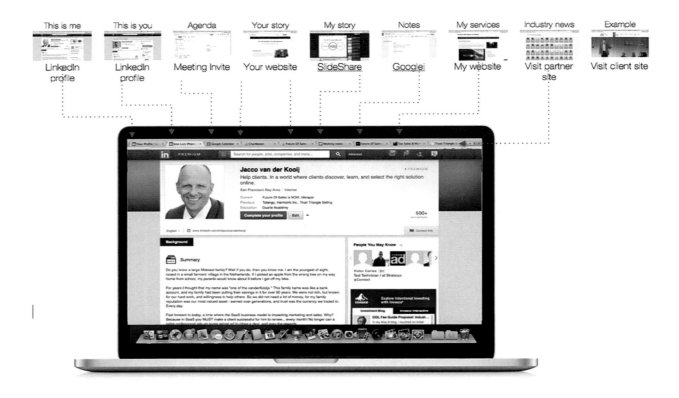

Figure 18: Tab-based selling

BEST PRACTICES

- **DO** practice!

- **DO** set up your tabs 15 minutes ahead of time.

- **DO NOT** exceed 10 tabs/window, you want to be able to read the headers.

- **DO** close all other apps + disable popup notifications.

- **DO** use a whiteboard, it works wonders!

- **DO** record the session to share with others.

- **DO** run your product/service demo in its own browser in case it crashes.

- **DO** pre-load a series of tabs in the right order, so the customer can expect what he will see.

- **DO** "surf" to examples your customer is bringing up; this further enhances the real-time experience, increasing the value – and with it, your credibility.

Summary

Process	WBD Play	Prepare
Communicate	**T** Tone	"Set the tone" Control your Speed, Pitch and Tone, etc.
	A Ask	Ask an open/closed- ended question to start the conversation.
	L Listen	Listen – the customer is going to give you hints – mirror them.
	K Keep notes	Keep brief notes – structure priority, relationship, tone.
	E Elaborate	Dig deeper – be curious with the intent to understand.
	R Repeat	Summarize what you thought the customer said.
Email	**R** Relevance	Prove you've researched or refer to others with similar context.
	R Reward	Offer value, such as a link to valuable insights, a relevant blog.
	R Request	Call to action based on situation (time, event, date etc.).

Voicemail	**W** Who are you	Hello my name is…
	W Why call	The reason I am reaching out is … I noticed that you.
	W WIIFM	**I was wondering if you like to.. ➔ EMAIL!**
Call	**W** Who, Why, WIIFM	Start off the call explaining who you are, why you're calling, and what's in it for the customer on this call.
	A Ask	Ask thoughtful questions based on research and insights.
	R Relevance	Don't pitch, make it about your customer.
	M Make it Happen	Set up clear, simple next steps.
Meeting elements	**1** Schedule	**Do not delay** - Does this afternoon work?
	2 Invite	Send out invite – Included executive briefing, monitor accepts.
	3 Confirm	Confirm 24hr/5mins. If more attendees, set up sponsor call.
	4 Prepare	
	5 Meet	Research. Customize. Sign-up. Download. Follow. Like. Share.
	6 Follow-up	**See next page**

Process	Plays	Prepare
Meeting structure		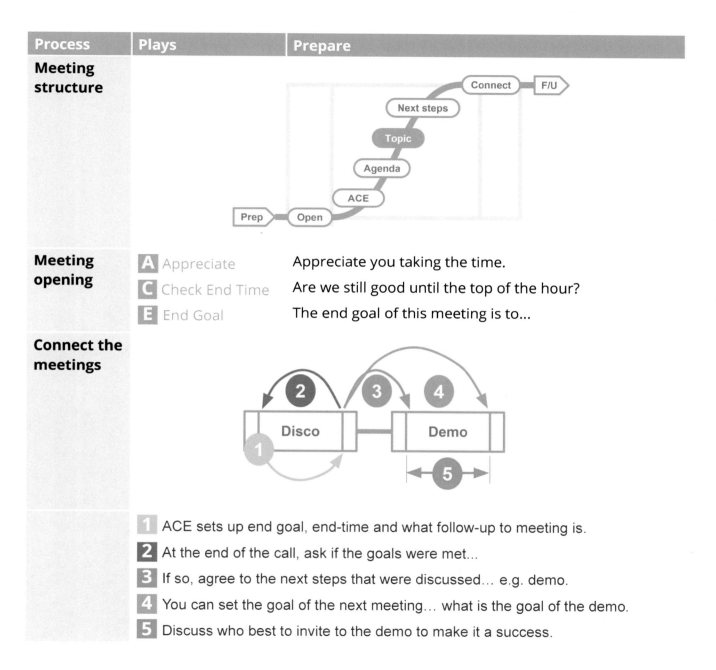
Meeting opening	**A** Appreciate	Appreciate you taking the time.
	C Check End Time	Are we still good until the top of the hour?
	E End Goal	The end goal of this meeting is to...
Connect the meetings		

1 ACE sets up end goal, end-time and what follow-up to meeting is.

2 At the end of the call, ask if the goals were met...

3 If so, agree to the next steps that were discussed... e.g. demo.

4 You can set the goal of the next meeting... what is the goal of the demo.

5 Discuss who best to invite to the demo to make it a success.

Conclusion

Each method of customer engagement we've discussed in this book seems simple on its surface. But the fact is that, whether you engage via voicemail, email, or in person, there are right and wrong ways of doing it! We encourage you to memorize the acronyms we've laid out for you here so that you can start off strong and then develop your own variations.

Abbreviations Used in this Book

People:
  AE: Account Executive
  AM: Account Manager
  BDR: Business Development Representative
  CSM: Customer Success Manager
  CEO: Chief Executive Officer
  CRO: Chief Revenue Officer
  CCO: Chief Customer Officer
  FAE: Field Account Executive
  MDR: Marketing Development Representative
  PM: Product Manager
  SDR: Sales Development Representative
  SE: Sales Engineer, sometimes refers to a web developer
  VPM: VP Marketing
  VPS: VP Sales

SaaS Lead Definition:
  Suspect: A person who may be interested
  Prospect: A person who expresses interest
  MQL: Marketing Qualified Lead, a person who expresses interest and fits the profile.
  SQL: Sales Qualified Lead, person who is interested
  SAL: Sales Accepted Lead
  WIN: A client who commits to the service
  LIVE: Client who has been onboarded

SaaS Business:
  ACV: Annual Contract Value
  ACRC: Annual Customer Retention Cost
  ARR: Annual Recurring Revenue equal to12 times MRR
  B2B: Business to Business
  B4B: Business for Business
  B2C: Business to Consumer

CAC: Client Acquisition Cost, the amount to acquire a single client
CR: Conversion Ratio, the amount of leads to produce one SQL
CRC: Client Retention Cost, the cost to retain a client for 12 months
CRM: Customer Relationship Management (platform)
CSM: Customer Success Management (platform)
ENT: Enterprises, companies with over 5,000 employees
LOGO: Common use term for a high-value client
LTV: Lifetime Value of a client, often between 3-5 times ACV
MAS: Marketing Automation Software (platform)
MRR: Monthly Recurring Revenue
PTC: Refers to the combined cost of (P)eople, (T)ools, and (C)ontent
RoI: Return on Investment
SaaS: Software as a Service
SC: Sales Cycle
SMB: Small to Medium Business(es) often between 50-500 employees
SME: Small to Medium Enterprise often between 500-5k employees
VSB: Very Small Business often between 2-50 employees
PRO: Prosumer, a single user who behaves like a business user
WR: Win Ratio, the number of accounts it takes to produce one WINIn the years since we published "Blueprints," we have been amazed at the response we have gotten from sales professionals in multiple fields, not just SaaS. It has been humbling!

About Winning By Design

Winning By Design was founded by Jacco Van Der Kooij with the purpose of helping SaaS companies level up their sales game in the face of radically compressed sales cycles and lower price points. We teach fundamental sales skills and combine them with process and systems to create self-teaching sales organizations.

To find out more about our offerings please visit:
www.saassalesmethod.com

Made in the USA
Monee, IL
23 April 2021